# The Left-Handed Hero

**BY MIIKO SHAFFIER**
co-written by Chana Grosser

Illustrated by: Dmitry Gitelman ( diemgi.com )
Layout & Design by: Ken Parker ( visual-variables.com )

Published by:
Shefer Publishing
**www.SheferPublishing.com**

For permissions, comments and ordering information write:
**Miiko@LearnHebrew.tv**

**ISBN 978-1-958999-01-1**

# THE LEFT-HANDED HERO

**an EASY EEVREET STORY**

BY MIIKO SHAFFIER

## SHEFER

PUBLISHING

*Based on Judges Chapter 3, verses 12-30.*
This story can be read like any English story book. When you get to a Hebrew word, do your best to sound it out and guess the meaning. You can check the pronunciation and meaning in the back of the book.

## HAVE FUN!

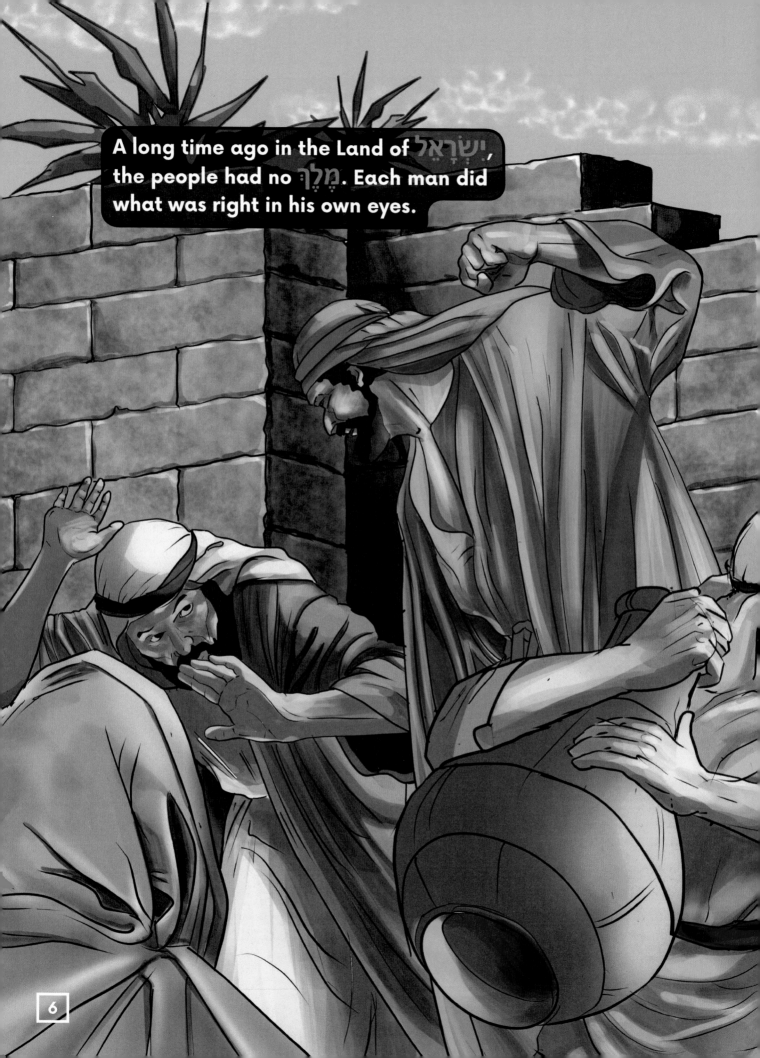

A long time ago in the Land of יִשְׂרָאֵל, the people had no מֶלֶךְ. Each man did what was right in his own eyes.

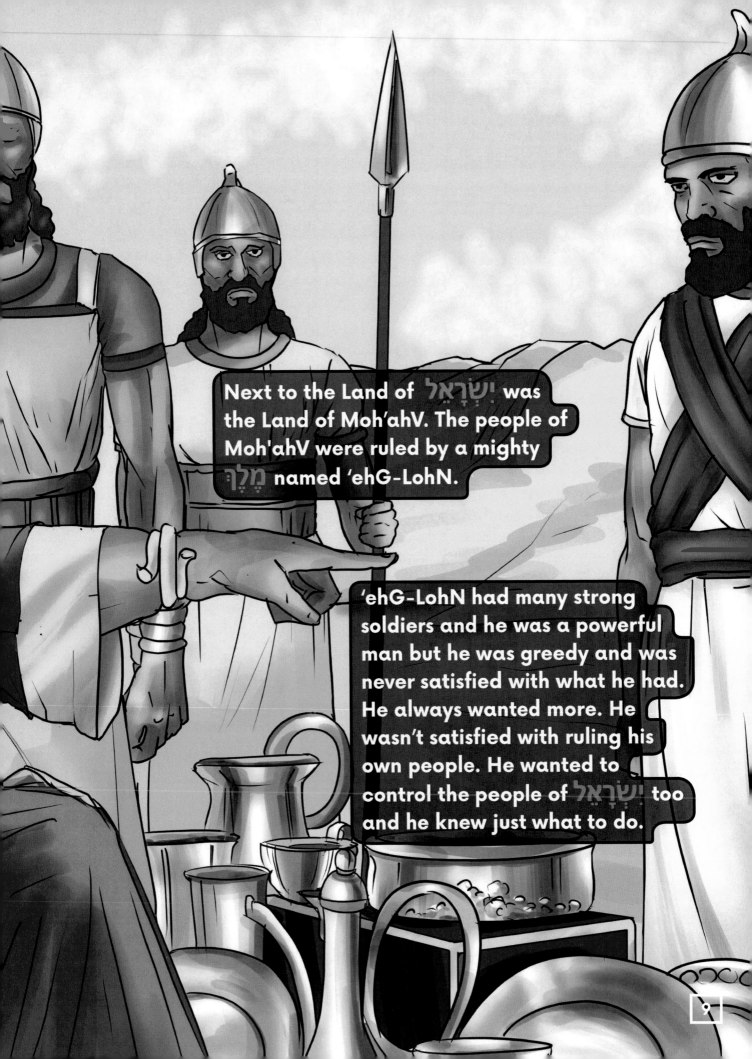

Next to the Land of יִשְׂרָאֵל was the Land of Moh'ahV. The people of Moh'ahV were ruled by a mighty מֶלֶךְ named 'ehG-LohN.

'ehG-LohN had many strong soldiers and he was a powerful man but he was greedy and was never satisfied with what he had. He always wanted more. He wasn't satisfied with ruling his own people. He wanted to control the people of יִשְׂרָאֵל too and he knew just what to do.

He hurried to carry out a wicked plan. 'ehG-LohN ganged up with his two neighbors. The מֶלֶךְ of 'ahMohN and the מֶלֶךְ of 'ahMahLehK. Together they were strong enough to fight and defeat the people of יִשְׂרָאֵל.

For a very long time 'ehG-LohN ruled the people with cruelty. They had to work for him and give the greedy מֶלֶךְ whatever he demanded. For שְׁמוֹנֶה עֶשְׂרֵה years they lived in fear and terror.

The people were suffering so much and they couldn't see any way out. They cried out for G-d's help. They remembered the one true G-d and they returned to His good ways.

Most people were right-handed and they fastened their חֶרֶב on their left יָרֵךְ. But אֵהוּד was left-handed! He could easily pull out his חֶרֶב from next to his right יָרֵךְ where no one expected a חֶרֶב to be.

אֵהוּד the new leader, had a bold and courageous plan. אֵהוּד made for himself a special חֶרֶב. It was a short חֶרֶב that was sharp on both sides. Now אֵהוּד was ready for an important secret mission!

אֵהוּד took with him a gift for מֶלֶךְ 'ehG-LohN. He was holding this gift as he walked the long journey to the palace.

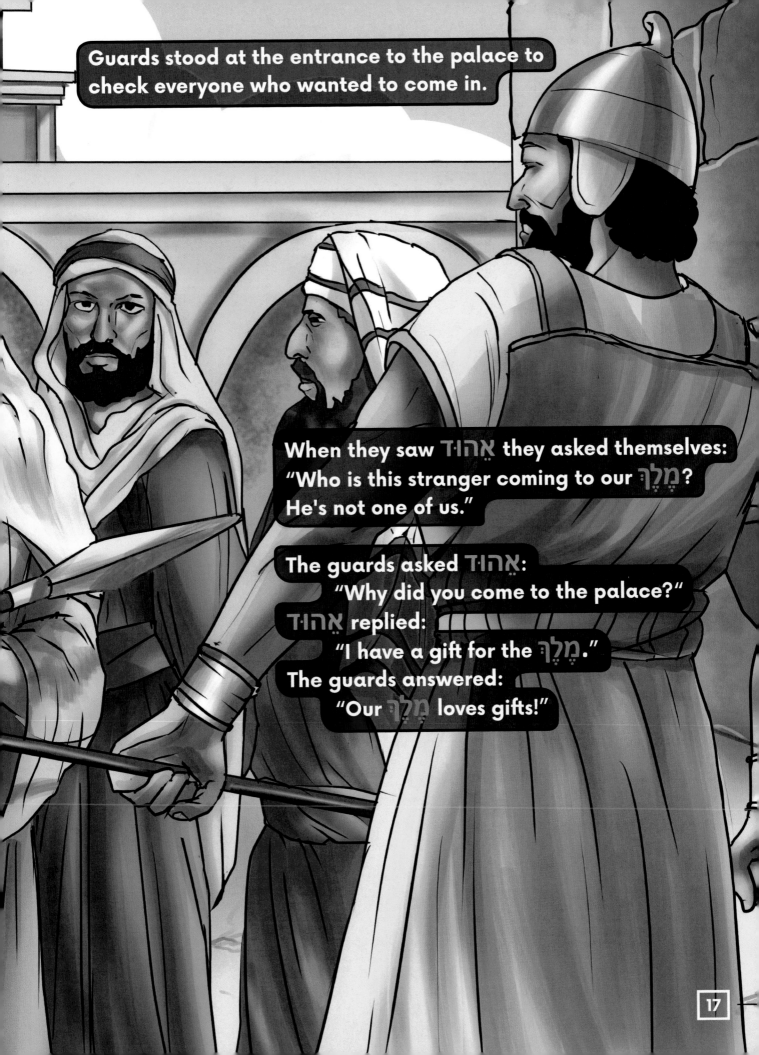

Guards stood at the entrance to the palace to check everyone who wanted to come in.

When they saw אֵהוּד they asked themselves: "Who is this stranger coming to our מֶלֶךְ? He's not one of us."

The guards asked אֵהוּד:
    "Why did you come to the palace?"
אֵהוּד replied:
    "I have a gift for the מֶלֶךְ."
The guards answered:
    "Our מֶלֶךְ loves gifts!"

17

The guards checked his left יָרֵךְ. They found no חֶרֶב there. They let אֵהוּד come in and move on.

When they saw אֵהוּד they asked themselves: "Who is this stranger coming to our מֶלֶךְ? He's not one of us."

The guards also asked אֵהוּד: "Why did you come to the palace? אֵהוּד replied: "I have a gift for the מֶלֶךְ." The guards answered: "Our מֶלֶךְ loves gifts!"

These guards checked his left יָרֵךְ as well. They found no חֶרֶב there. They let אֵהוּד come in and move on.

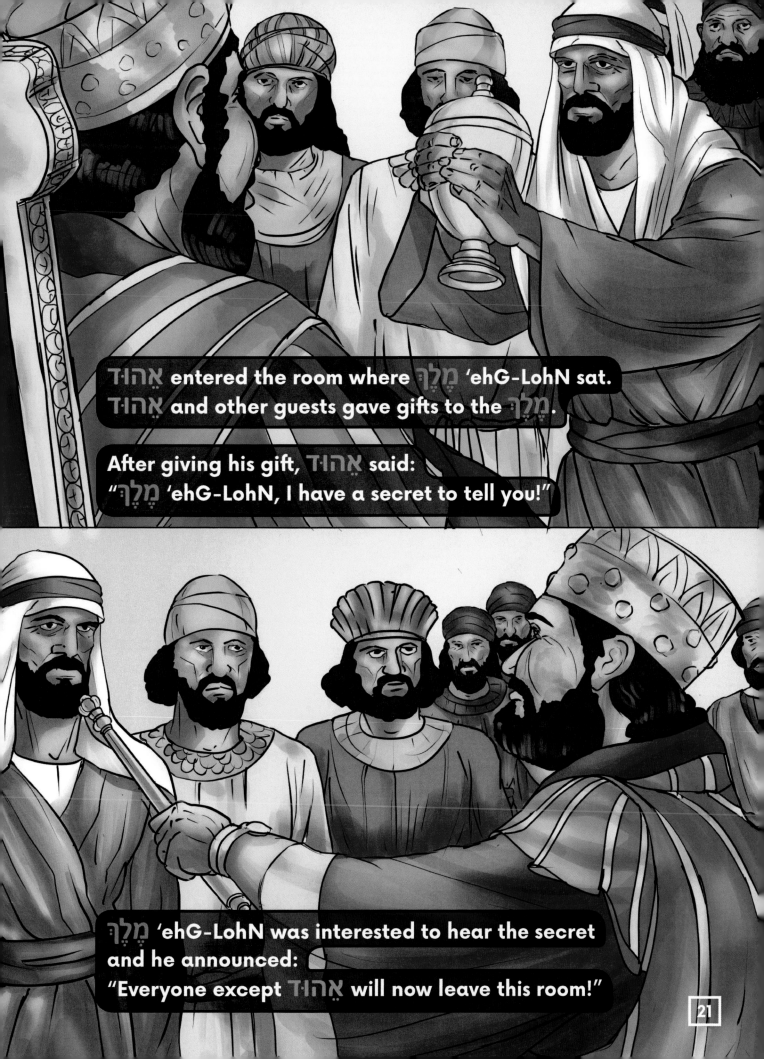

אֵהוּד entered the room where מֶלֶךְ 'ehG-LohN sat. אֵהוּד and other guests gave gifts to the מֶלֶךְ.

After giving his gift, אֵהוּד said:
"מֶלֶךְ 'ehG-LohN, I have a secret to tell you!"

מֶלֶךְ 'ehG-LohN was interested to hear the secret and he announced:
"Everyone except אֵהוּד will now leave this room!"

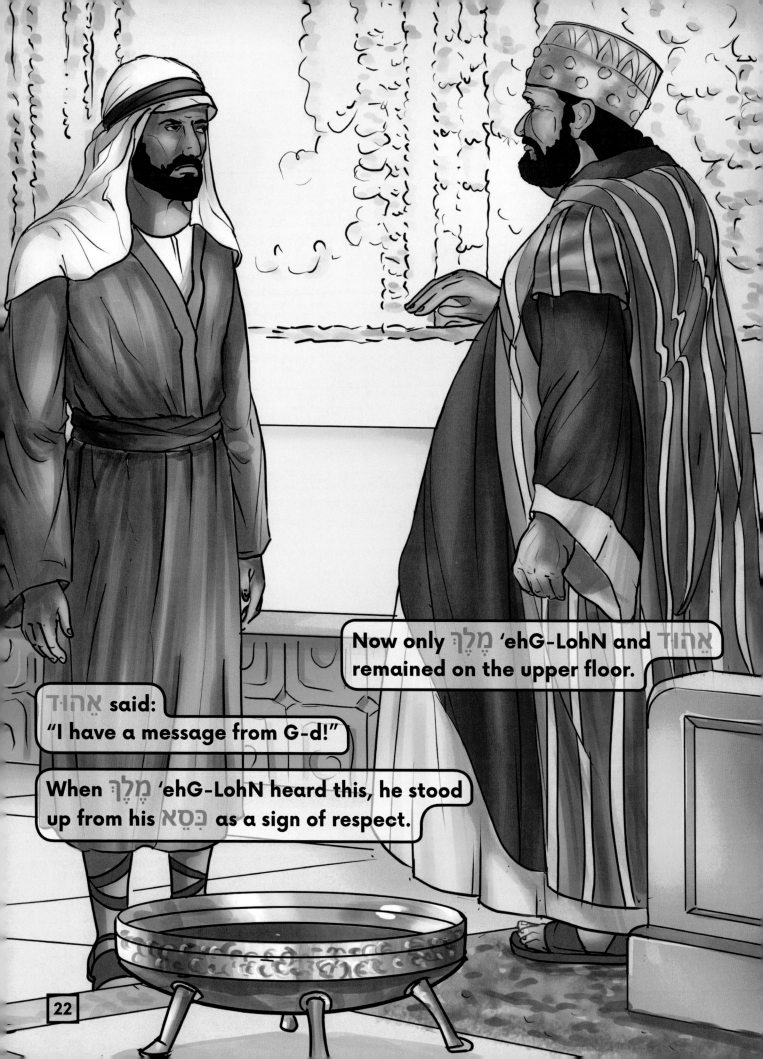

Now only מֶלֶךְ 'ehG-LohN and אֵהוּד remained on the upper floor.

אֵהוּד said:
"I have a message from G-d!"

When מֶלֶךְ 'ehG-LohN heard this, he stood up from his כִּסֵא as a sign of respect.

Right then, our hero אֵהוּד swiftly reached his left hand to his right יֶרֶךְ. He took his short חֶרֶב, and plunged it into מֶלֶךְ 'ehG-LohN. Even the handle of the חֶרֶב disappeared into 'ehG-LohN's immense belly.

'ehG-LohN, the wicked מֶלֶךְ was dead!

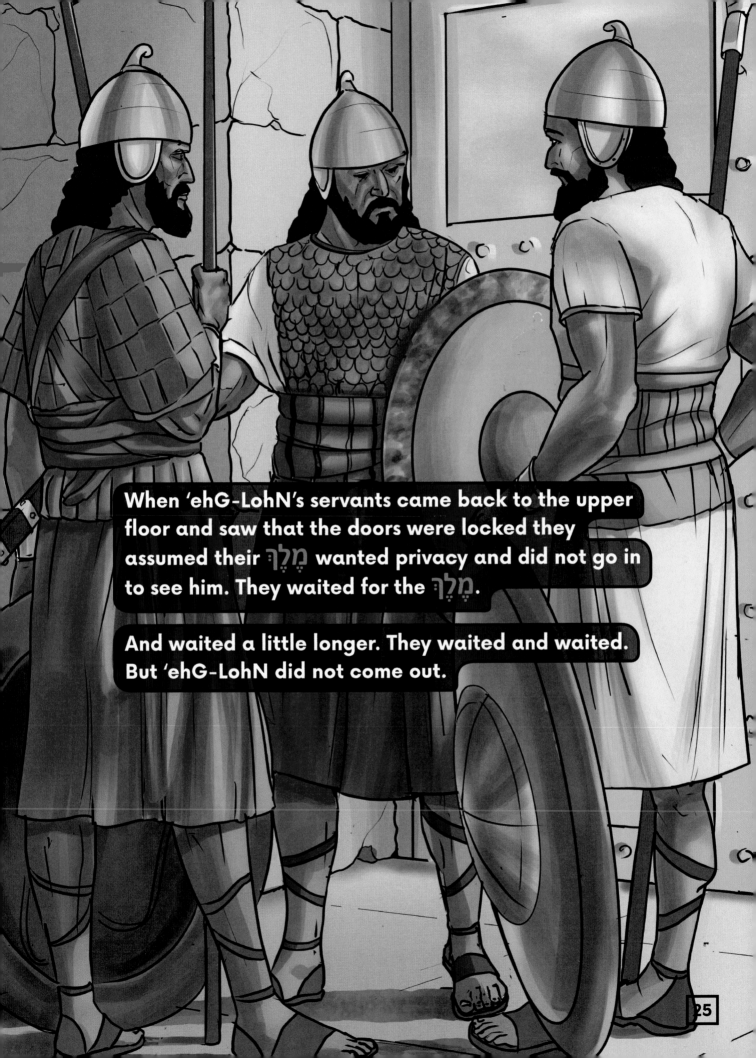

When 'ehG-LohN's servants came back to the upper floor and saw that the doors were locked they assumed their מֶלֶךְ wanted privacy and did not go in to see him. They waited for the מֶלֶךְ.

And waited a little longer. They waited and waited. But 'ehG-LohN did not come out.

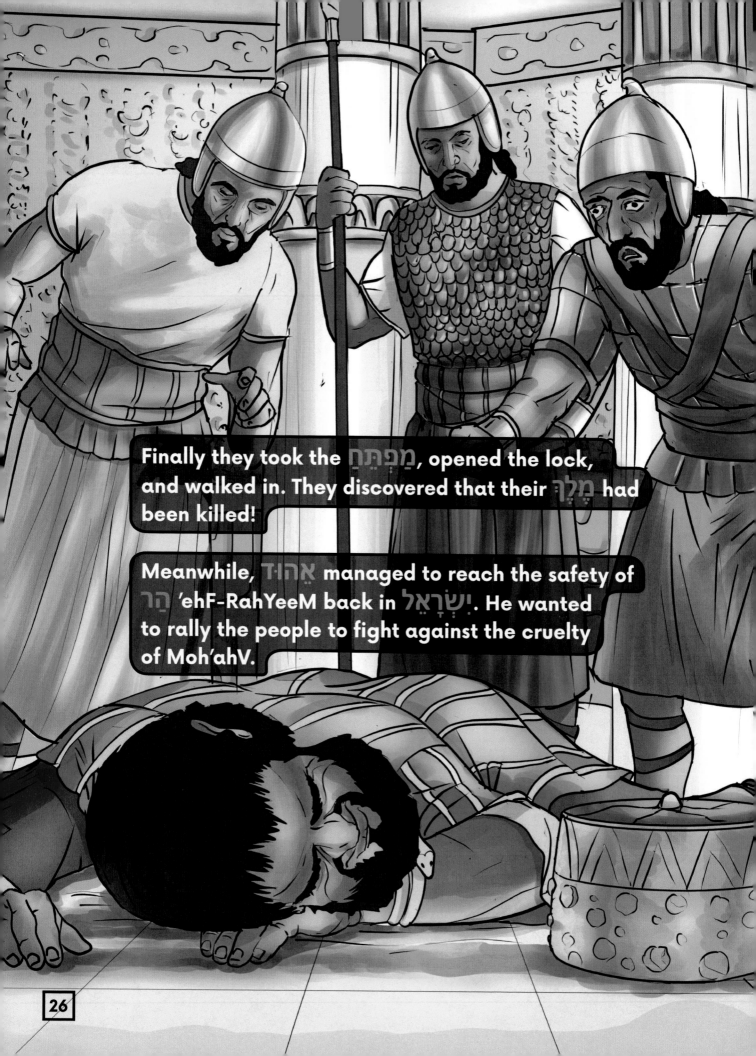

Finally they took the מַפְתֵּחַ, opened the lock, and walked in. They discovered that their מֶלֶךְ had been killed!

Meanwhile, אֵהוּד managed to reach the safety of 'ehF-RahYeeM back in יִשְׂרָאֵל הַר. He wanted to rally the people to fight against the cruelty of Moh'ahV.

But how could he call them? אֵהוּד knew just what to do - אֵהוּד blew the shofar! אֵהוּד blew, and blew.

Every blow announced: Come fight with me! We can win! Join me! Don't be afraid! G-d is with us!

The people of יִשְׂרָאֵל joined their leader אֵהוּד. Together they captured the crossings of the YahR-DehN River that led to the Land of Moh'ahV. They fought Moh'ahV's strongest soldiers and not one of the soldiers of Moh-ahV escaped.

**Here are the Hebrew words from this *Easy Eevreet Story*:**

יִשְׂרָאֵל

YeeS-Rah'ehL – **ISRAEL** | p. 6,9,10,26,28,29

מֶלֶךְ

MehLehCH – **KING** | p. 6,9-11,15,17,19, 20-23,25,26

שְׁמוֹנֶה עֶשְׂרֶה

SH-MohNehH 'ehS-RehH – **18** | p. 11

SH-MohNehH means eight and 'ehS-RehH means ten.
Together they mean eighteen.

אִישׁ

'eeYSH – **MAN** | p. 12

חַיִל

CHahYeeL – **COURAGE** | p. 12

אִישׁ חַיִל  'eeYSH CHahYeeL – **MAN (OF) COURAGE OR HERO.**

אֵהוּד

'ehHooD– **EHUD** | p. 12-15,17,18-24, 26-29

חֶרֶב

CHehRehV – **SWORD** | p. 13,14,18,20,23

יֶרֶךְ

YehRehCH – **THIGH** | p. 14,18,20,23

This story talks about the numbers 18 and 80. In the Easy Eevreet story called *The Miracle at Jericho* we learned numbers one through ten. Let's learn some more **numbers!**

**11** אַחַת עֶשְׂרֵה
'ehCHahT 'ehS-RehH

**12** שְׁתֵּים עֶשְׂרֵה
SH-TehYM 'ehS-RehH

**13** שְׁלוֹשׁ עֶשְׂרֵה
SH-LohSH 'ehS-RehH

**14** אַרְבַּע עֶשְׂרֵה
'ahR-Bah' 'ehS-RehH

**15** חֲמֵשׁ עֶשְׂרֵה
CHahMehSH 'ehS-RehH

**16** שֵׁשׁ עֶשְׂרֵה
SHehSH 'ehS-RehH

**17** שְׁבַע עֶשְׂרֵה
SH-Vah' 'ehS-RehH

**18** שְׁמוֹנֶה עֶשְׂרֵה
SH-MohNehH 'ehS-RehH

**19** תְּשַׁע עֶשְׂרֵה
T-SHah' 'ehS-RehH

**You did it!** Take a deep breath, shake your fingers and get ready for the next set. **Let's go!**

 עֶשְׂרִים
'ehS-ReeYM

 שְׁלוֹשִׁים
SH-LohSHeeYM

 אַרְבָּעִים
ahR-Bah'eeYM

 חֲמִשִּׁים
CHahMeeSHeeYM

שִׁשִּׁים
SHeeSHeeYM

 שִׁבְעִים
SHeeV-'eeYM

שְׁמוֹנִים
SH-MohNeeYM

תִּשְׁעִים
TeeSH-'eeYM

מֵאָה
Meh'ahH

I hope you loved this story and will have a good time practicing your new Hebrew words. You can start right away by offering a כִּסֵּא to someone visiting your home, and helping your mother fold that הַר of clean laundry. Or you can lay on your back like a מֶלֶךְ and count the clouds or the stars.

# Hi!

My name is **Miiko**. I live in Be'er Sheva, Israel. My husband Aaron and I have nine kids: Menucha, Mendel, Dovi, Yisroel, Freida, Devora, Fitche, Geula, and Azaria.

I teach Hebrew reading with a fun little book called *Learn to Read Hebrew in 6 Weeks!*

My second book *The Hebrew Workbook* teaches readers to write in Hebrew.

*The Left-Handed Hero* is part of a series of storybooks that teach Hebrew vocabulary to kids.

I'm so pleased to be a part of your Hebrew journey. If you have any questions or want to say hi please send me an email! **Miiko@LearnHebrew.tv**

# To the Parents

This book is designed to teach Hebrew vocabulary to people who already know how to read the Hebrew alphabet. While reading this Bible story in English you'll come across Hebrew words embedded in the text. Sound out the words and try to guess their meaning from the context. Check the key in the back of the book to see if you were right.

I've chosen to transliterate the names of the biblical characters mentioned in this story so that you'll learn the authentic Hebrew pronunciation of these biblical names.

## Transliteration

*The Left-Handed Hero* uses the same system of transliteration as my first book *Learn to Read Hebrew in 6 Weeks!*

I came up with a unique transliteration system. It's designed to have the reader pronouncing the Hebrew words accurately without ever having heard a Hebrew speaker pronounce those words.

**Here's a breakdown of the system:**

Each consonant is represented as a capital letter and each vowel by small letters.

The silent letters 'ahLehF (א) and 'ahYeeN (ע) are represented by an apostrophe (')

The silent vowel 'Sh-Vah' (:) is represented as a hyphen (-).

An important exception to make note of:
The CH does not represent the ch sound like in *chair* or *chest*. In fact, Hebrew doesn't have the ch sound like *chair* or *chest* at all.

The CH represents the letters CHehT(ח) and CHahF(כ) and Final ChahF(ך). These letters make a sound not found in the English language. It's a chokey sound that almost sounds like a kitten purring but much harsher. Think about the name of the composer Bach. From what my Spanish speaking students tell me, it's the same sound as the guttural J in Spanish.

Let's look at the first word in the Hebrew Scripture as an example of how my system works:

בְּרֵאשִׁית

I transliterate it:
B-Reh'SHeeYT

Others may transliterate Bereshit or Bresheet but then you wouldn't know if the vowels are long or short.

If you learned to read Hebrew using my other book, you are already well familiar with this system. But in case you learned to read Hebrew elsewhere, here's a key to make sure it's clear.

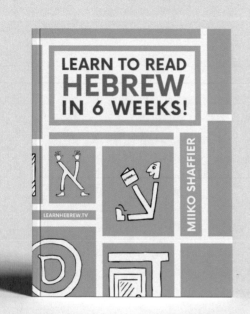
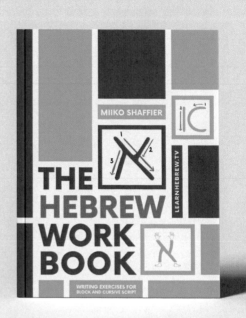